Life Happens Poetry

ROSE C. MAY-TALLMAN

BALBOA.
PRESS

A DIVISION OF HAY HOUSE

Scripture taken from the New King James Version®. Copyright ©
1982 by Thomas Nelson. Used by permission. All rights reserved.

Balboa Press books may be ordered through
booksellers or by contacting:

Balboa Press
A Division of Hay House
1663 Liberty Drive
Bloomington, IN 47403
www.balboapress.com
1 (877) 407-4847

Because of the dynamic nature of the Internet, any web
addresses or links contained in this book may have changed
since publication and may no longer be valid. The views
expressed in this work are solely those of the author and do
not necessarily reflect the views of the publisher, and the
publisher hereby disclaims any responsibility for them.

The author of this book does not dispense medical advice or
prescribe the use of any technique as a form of treatment for physical,
emotional, or medical problems without the advice of a physician,
either directly or indirectly. The intent of the author is only to offer
information of a general nature to help you in your quest for emotional
and spiritual well-being. In the event you use any of the information
in this book for yourself, which is your constitutional right, the
author and the publisher assume no responsibility for your actions.

Any people depicted in stock imagery provided by Thinkstock are
models, and such images are being used for illustrative purposes only.
Certain stock imagery © Thinkstock.

Print information available on the last page.

ISBN: 978-1-5043-8357-8 (sc)
ISBN: 978-1-5043-8358-5 (e)

Library of Congress Control Number: 2017910122

Balboa Press rev. date: 07/17/2017

Contents

Dedication

I want to thank God, Savior, and Holy Spirit for inspiring me to write this book.

My husband Terry and my three sons Greg, Matt, Frank for inspiration. My granddaughter Katie, who encouraged me to finish the book. Joe, my loving, fun brother, and his wonderful wife Danielle. My sister Julia and granddaughter Sophia who are the main reason for the title "Life Happens Poetry".

I would also like to thank my very best friend Joan for helping me through all the good and rough times in my life. She has been a strong source of encouragement and strength even during many difficult times of her life.

To my kindhearted grandson Matthew; who is with our Lord. He was so strong and brave. He is an example of how we all should live and die. With love, peace, grace, and dignity.

Also, my cousin Sandy, aunt Mattie and my mother's best friend Faye; These are three of the most amazing women I have ever known. They have given and gave most of their life helping other people and God's children.

Introduction

I have lead quite the colorful life! The poems were inspired by twist and turns my life has taken and through people I have met along life's journey. Holy Spirit inspired a few poems. (See if you can find the Holy Spirit's inspired poems.)

Because of these twists and turns, some of these poems are light hearted while others seem very dark.

The title was created from some family members talking about anxiety all the time. I cannot stand the word anxiety! Because it just adds more worry to what people are already worried about. At least that is what it does to me. So, when life happens; I just pray and try to give my worries to Jesus.

Everyone has difficulties during their journey through life on earth and we can only hope to enjoy the peace that grace brings through Jesus Christ.

I hope you find comfort in "Life Happens Poetry" knowing you are not along in your journeys through life.

May grace and peace be multiplied to you through in knowledge of God and of Jesus Christ our Lord. (NKJV 2 Peter 1:2)

Angels Calling Me Home

Mom! I hear Angels all around me!
I see Angels dancing around me,
And they want me to come out and dance.
But, I hear your warm sweet voice,
As you whisper in my ear.
Mom, can I please go dance with them?

I hear Angels all around me,
And they're wanting me to come out and play.
But, I feel your soft embrace,
And something warm fell on my face.
Mom, May I please go out and play.

There are Angels calling my name,
And they want me to go home with them.
I don't really want to go.
But, it's time for me to leave.
Mom, I'm going to my new home.

I'm dancing with Angels in my new home,
And I want you to know; that I'm okay.
For there is not any pain up here,
And a lot of love to go around.
Mom, Jesus is holding me now!

There are Angels playing in my new home,
And we can't wait to show you around.

We have so much love here,
And no one ever goes without.
Mom, we're watching over you, now!

I have been with Angels all my life,
And the greatest one of all is you.
In the world that I was born in,
Mom, I would have never known love.
But because of you, in a few shorts months; I knew.

Mom, always remember, I Love You!

Arms Open Wide

Picture the Lord walking on the rough water.
Arms opened wide, walking toward you.
Can you hear Him, with the voice of an angel?
Calling your name to come too!

Do you have the faith that God gave a small seed?
Faith and trust are what you need to walk on water.
That's what it takes to become a disciple.
Would you answer Him now?

Peter and Paul had the faith of an oak tree.
But they both still stumbled and fell.
Then they picked themselves up
and ask for forgiveness.
Could you believe in Him now?

So, get down on your knees like the human you are,
Arms open wide, He's walking to you.
Do you have the faith to pick yourself
up and ask for forgiveness?

I'm down on my knees asking for
faith not to stumbled.
Arms opened wide without any doubts.
And that is what it takes to become a disciple.
I will walk to Him, now!

Would you run to Him now?
Put all your faith in Him!
What have you got to lose?

Come Home

You were not here to see me laugh,
You were not the here to play with me,
You were not here to hold me when I cried.
You were not here to watch me graduate.

Someday I will be older, laughing and
playing with someone else.
Someday I will be happy and all
my tears will go away.

Someday, God will hear my prayers
and bring you back to me.

Dance of Seasons

It's spring and the trees are starting to sprout.
But, I can only see branches of gray.
They do not show their outside joy.
Until the dull gray no longer shows.
Then they danced in the wind to the glory of spring.

It's summer now and the trees are so excited,
In all their glory of different shades of green.
They danced to the breeze of wind and rain.
God saw their glory within the dance,
All sadness was forgotten with each dance.

Autumn with her beauty brought rustic colors.
The trees ended their dancing and
prepare for Winter's touch.
The trees changed to a red, yellow
and orange delight,
And in the mystic magic; I saw
their majesty and glory.
A beauty so defined, that no human could design.

I see the shiver of the trees on Winter's coldest day.
I wondered how they stayed alive
and birds of every prey,
Were sheltered in the trees that God did create.
I saw the ice, snow and wind burn
each branch from within.
Though torture, the trees stood strong and bold.

Rose C. May-Tallman

It's Spring again and the trees are starting to sprout.
This time, I see the branches not gray at all,
But, showing off the newborn
spring with each sprout.

Glory to God in the highest who created us all!
So, with faith and nobility we shall never fall!

Drug Addict's-Fields of Pain and Grace

Stranded without help!
Buckled under with loneliness and hurt,
My refuge of money is depleted,
The one I love cannot release her past.
Darkness consumes me,

Nowhere to go,
Too old to turn back.
Scared of losing everything.
But nothing lasts forever!
Where should I begin?

Mom, says, begin with completely
surrendering to Jesus.
Forget about losing earthy things.
We were not created to serve self, women and men.

She says, peace comes in having Faith.
She says, comfort comes in having Hope.
She says, negative thoughts cause,
pain, chaos, and catastrophes.
She says, let go, let God!
She says, Faith leads to earthly and eternal Grace.

It's hard to believe in what she says.
When all I see in my life causes me hurt.

She says, we create our earthly pain,
And God lets it happen,
Because He's trying to get our attention.
So, He can help us.

Peace and healing comes with complete surrender,
Peace and healing comes in trusting
God's grace and promises.
Peace come with obedience and prayer.

She asks, "What's your mission
here on earth for God"?
She asks, "How are you going to get there"?

Mom say's, Total surrender to Jesus is the only way.
Jesus will heal you and take you to great places.
Places you will find it hard to believe that
it is you leading a normal life serving,
honoring, and glorifying God.

Excuses

If the Savior was standing before me now.
What excuses could I make?

The days are too short.
The family expects too much.
The bills are too many to pay.

I'm sorry, I did not take time to pray.

Could you forgive me for what I
have NOT done today?

If the Savior was standing before us,
What excuses could we make.

Fairy War

I awoke to find a fairy war,
I could not believe my eyes!
Beautiful colors and wings,
Fighting in the sky.

To my amazement, they did not bleed,
But as they fell, they disappeared.
Leaving only wooden swords,
To show they were here.

I pick-up the wooden swords,
And as I turned to walk away,
Laughing merrily and playing,
All the beautiful fairies reappeared!

Faith

With wings, we fly,
With grace, we pray,
And with faith we soar.

Faith-Never Trust What Men May Say

Put your faith were with belongs,
Put you trust in God alone.
Help yourself to find the way,
Do not trust what men may say.

Never wait until tomorrow,
Never complain about your sorrows.
Shine your light your own way.
Never trust what men may say.

Always listen to the wind,
You will always find a friend.
A whispering voice will lead the way.
Never trust what men may say.

When you're feeling all alone.
And no one seems to be at home.
Put your faith where it belongs.
Put your faith in God alone.

Faith, Prayers, And Grace

When I feel temptation following me,
I turn my head and close my eyes,
I know it's Christ standing by my side.

The road I traveled has not been easy,
Long and lonely many days,
I sit in my room and pray.

I know the road may be long,
The way maybe hard and lonely,
But, I've never been alone.

It's hard to believe in what cannot be seen.
When faith and grace is all you have.
But we can move mountains with our Faith.

And with prayers,
Every prayer heard can be answered.
And every disease can be healed!

With Grace, broken hearts can be mended.
Through Faith, we can find our way,
And through Prayers, God will take
us to where He wants us to be!

Finding Myself

Oh, the pain in my mind.
Nothingness wondering wild.
Never knowing what to do.
Never doing what I should.

Sadness inside and out.
Dark clouds hanging all around.
Never finding myself,
Never seeing who I really am.

Running away from my thoughts,
Through endless happy tales.
Never believing in today.
Never looking for tomorrow.

People running my life.
Me laying around closing my eyes.
Never saying "NO" to others problems.
Never saying "YES" to new adventures.

Trying to let go and let God,
Trying to find God's perfect plan.
Never listing to my heart.
Never hearing God's soft voice.

Now, I ask the Lord above,
Have mercy on me that I may hear,
Never giving up on God's plan.
Never giving up on me.

God Never Promised Us
Silver and Pearls

If you're waiting for that big break,
It's not going to come to you in your state of mind.
You must get off that couch,
And find your heart's desires,
God never promised us silver and pearls.

When your pockets are empty and
your bills are overdue,
And you don't have a dime to give.
Just remember others before you,
And how they struggled to give to you.
God never promised us silver and pearls.

Through trials and tribulations.
I've wondered many roads.
But faith and grace have helped me,
To make it safely home.
God never promised us silver and pearls.

If you are laying down cold and wondering,
And you hear your name being called.
No one else around has heard a voice call at all.
Just remember to answer God's call.

Rose C. May-Tallman

God doesn't come calling with silver and pearls.
Silver you must work hard for,
And pearls you need to dive deep for,
The harder you work and the deeper you dive,
The more you are going to learn.

If You Blame God

If your troubles are heavy.
And your worries are deep,
But He isn't listening.
SO, YOU THINK!!

What have you done to help yourself?
If you pray for help and receive none,
What have you done for God?

If you pray for money because bills are overdue,
How much have you given to Him?
What have you got to lose?

If your house needs repairs with no money to spare.
Stop and think!
What have you done to help God's house?

Your children need food, assistance you must have.
When you had money,
Did you feed God's children too?

Your brother stole something of yours,
Did you forgive him?
If not, why should God forgive you?

You think church is a joke,
Money, they want!
How long have you stayed in one
long enough to know?

You get drunk, you do drugs and wonder around,
You see no light at the end of town,
And you wonder why, God has treated you so bad!

My friend; re-read what you just read!
God is waiting on you to stop
doing what you are doing!
So, He can step in and help!

If you still wonder why God is not there,
God is waiting on you to open your heart and mind.
To receive Him in your heart to
let Him know you care.

Little Rose

One day there was a little boy,
As cute as he cute be.
He like to steal toys,
And other things, you see!

One day he wondered far away,
And found a little Rose.
He picked it and ran with it,
As fast as he could go.

And as the story goes,
He laid it down one day;
And when he wasn't looking,
Someone stole his little Rose.

So, the little boy was very sad,
And then, he found out!
The little Rose just ran off to grow!
So, he was very glad!

Have a good day!
From one thief to another!

The First Little Rose

My Prayer

Jesus, I praise you for this day
and every day to come.
Lord, thank you for all you do!

May your will be done in our lives.
Guide and lead us in Your ways, not ours.

May Your glorious will be a light in all I do.
Keep and guide me from temptation.

Guard my heart against people and things
that may lead me away from You.

Protect me from satan and all he sends that
may infer with your wonderful plan.

Praise Your love and your kindness
forever and always.

AMEN

Never Noticing

The sun is shining all around.
People too busy to hear the sounds,
Rushing and pushing along life's streets,
Never noticing all the people stepping on their feet.

Did you notice the sun shining all around?
Were you too busy to hear the sounds?
Were you one of the crowd, pushing others down?
Did you notice people, when you
stepped on their feet?

Path to Home

I started down the road, following my Savior.

I followed Him a little way, and then, I got
uncomfortable and life didn't seem the same.

I came to a turn in the road; I saw a stranger
standing there, who looked tempting and fun.
I took the turn, and started following, -- following the
stranger; on the road that was rough and tattered.

I stumbled and fell on the road; on
this road that never ended.
I was bruised and worn, weak and
broken. Wish life would end.

Then I looked up and saw my Savior,
standing there once again.
He held out His hand and I ask for His forgiveness.

Lord, I'm sorry I left you alone.
He said, "But you were never left alone.
I was here with you all along. All you had to
do was take my hand and follow me home.

So, I took His hand and He lifted me up.
I turned around and walked back.
And saw that the path was a much brighter one.

Leading to the Kingdom; Leading to home.

I can't say it was easy! There were many struggles.
I stumbled and fell; He picked
me up. I stumbled again.

There were times I was worn and tattered.
But He was there to pick me up and give me rest.

"On the path to home."

And someday when I get there, I
know, I will not be alone.
Cause Christ has always been there with
me, walking on the "Path to Home".

He never said, 'Life would be easy.
He said, "He would always be with me."

Even though sometimes, I let him down,
and forgot who I was, and who He is.
He never let me down and never left me.

Now, I remember where I belong;
In the arms of my Savior,
taking His hand and walking towards home.

Rush

It's cold outside and I wonder why,
People hurry all the while,
Don't they know that life is too short?
They rush around without a choice.

No feelings for others they see each day,
Can you believe, what I say?
They don't take time to stop and pray,
They rush around without a care.

Minds a whirling making plans,
Not stopping to play for a moment, my friend!
Just plan, work and pay the bills,
They rush around without any of life's thrills.

Today, I stopped and wondered why?
I just let so much of life past me by.
Work, eat and sleep, all the while,
Rushing around without a smile.

Snow-Snow

It's early, it's cold,
I'm tired of the snow!
Hurrying around to make these planes go.
Watching my step where ever I go.

Special Thanks

I would like to give you many things.
But, the moon was too high for me to reach,
And even if I could reach the sun; it would be hot!

The ocean is too far away,
And if I could catch a cloud in a jar,
It would only disappear.

There are many things I would like to give you,
But most of these gifts are already in view.

So, here's a special THANK YOU!
For all your encouragement,
For all your help throughout the years.

Thank you very much from my mind and my heart!

Sun Dancing

I saw the sun dancing in and out
of silver lined clouds.
She peaked between orange layers
of mountains proud!

As her beauty showed through heavenly holes,
Sunbeams tried to touch the ground below.

A playground of pink cotton balls,
If I were light enough; I would run across them all!

To meet the sun before she bowed down;
To greet the night light of the moon so proud.

Survive

To survive in the wilderness,
One must know how to fight.

To survive in the world,
One must learn how to fight.

To survive in Heaven,
One must learn how to die.

The Watching Wolf

He does not care for his children or mine,
He prays with the wicked howling in the night.
He fears the Eagle, the Lion, and the Bear,
But stakes our children in the night air.

Hunters are searching for him day and night.
But only one has true sight.

The wolf is hiding in the grass,
Although, I can never see his eyes.
I can feel his gaze as he slowly walks by.

He does not care who I am,
No one can understand!

So, Sleep lightly my friend,

The wolf will strike quick,
With-in the twinkling of an eye!
We all should be ready,
To take shelter or fight!

Through His Death

Through His Death
Destruction will not be.
But love and peace are our reward.

Through His Death
Chaos will be no more,
We will be at peace with the world.

Through His Death
We will soar like birds.
Pain and suffering will be gone.

Free will be free!

Through His Death
Tears of war will be no more.
We will see the world at peace.

Through His Death
We will learn to be ourselves.
We will be free from worldly things.

Through His Death
If we can accept His grace.
We will be free and at peace.

Through His Death and Resurrection,
We will see a new Earth.
Praise be to Father, Son, and Holy Ghost.

Today's Storm of Life

Tis a long stormy day and I can only tell,
If life is drifting by like the ocean carries shells.
I sit and I wonder; if the journey
through life is too short?
But to my disbelief! we can never touch the sky!

Not thinking about tomorrow or what lays ahead,
We rush through every moment,
never thinking of the dead.
But today I sit and marveled at the things in my life.
What wonders God has given me in this short time.

Have I traveled life's road too
quickly? I really don't think so!
Or have the ocean waves so strongly
washed me to shore?
The storm outside is windy and loud.
But, there is peace in the soul that never grows old.

So, my friends, when you're looking for tomorrow,
Don't rush through life's gates to find sorrow.
Sit and watch the storms, and
what they might bring.
For the calming after a storm, is
a most enjoyable thing.

The Tragedy-Part One

I lost the one I love so much,
She left without even a hunch!
I cannot live without her insight,
I cannot live without her in my life!

I wish I could call someone,
Talk it over and let it go.
My thoughts of her are very strong.
My minds the devil that won't let go!

She packed her bags and walked away,
My mind is fried; I can't get her to stay!
I feel I'm leading a double life.
I wish I did not know how to cry!

Death would be easier than this,
Hell, it does exist!
Without her; I want to die.
Life would be nicer on the other side.

My mother and my friends would understand,
I would not be an unhappy man.
It will be better on the other side.
Pain and hurt would not make me cry.

Mom, this is not a tragedy.
You will be better off without this sad son.
One that is always depressed,
Because of a woman that left so fast!

Death is not just a grave,
I believe, it's a new way,
To get away from this earthly pain.
I don't think, I'll be afraid!

DON'T FORGET TO READ THE OUTCOME!
"THE TRAGEDY-PART 2"
NEXT PAGE

The Tragedy-Part Two

I woke up to find a new day,
I knew death was not far away.
I laid and I watched as people passed by.
So many of them, why are they crying?

Don't they know I'm resting now?
No more earthy pain or shame.
No lost love to be my blame.
Why can't I find "peace" in this crowd?

There is my mother, she dressed in black!
Mom, it's me, please don't look back.
I did not mean to make you cry.
I did not want to say good-bye.

Dad, why are you sitting so quietly?
Don't you know; I really did care!
I'm so sorry for what I've done.
Will you forgive this unhappy son?

Julie, we worked so close for so long,
I did not know your love was so strong,
I wish you had told me how you felt.
Maybe your love would have set me free!

Now I see; we both are lost.
Please do not do what I have done.
I was the selfish one.
That took away your love for me.

Death has come to take me now,
My sad judgement, I must face.
I can see the fires of hell,
Filled with shame and disgrace.

Death is not just a grave,
I believe I could have found another way.
To take away the earthly pain,
Now believe what I say; I'm so afraid!!

True Friends

Most friends are like runaway trains,
They leave at once without any shame.
They find someone else with a little more fame.
And next they'll hurt them with their uncouth game.

I found this true with most I've met,
Friends do not come in groups or in pairs,
They are quite rare as red fur on hares,
Friend do not embarrass you with their filth.

True friends share your every joy and pain.
They would not hurt you for silver or gold.
They will not hurt you for fame of old!
They are more previous than
the largest pot of Gold!

I had three true friends in my life up to now,
The rest are family which are
worth more, you know.
One went away to join our Lord,
One lives far, but calls when I speak his name.
And one sits across from me at work each day.

The rest you know are like runaway trains,
Trying to find themselves in a world full of fame.
Never really meaning to hurt anyone,
But they like good times, power, and fame.

So, guard your hearts and souls my friends,
Because this is as close as I will ever
let these people get to me again!

Untamed Desires

I can see what you are like,
Behind the fun and dynamite,
With all the jesters, you imply,
You don't think; I know your mind!

How can so many be such fools,
Believing and trusting in all you do!
A few trips and glasses of wine,
Do you not know; your own mind?

I saw you standing next to her,
Your arms around her very near,
You act so incense and pure,
Do you like these games, My Dear?

I don't need these feelings in my mind,
Wrapped up with pain and desire,
The world you live in is your own,
Your thoughts are not of me alone.

Selfish and greed are yours,
Hidden behind the pain you endure,
I wish I did not know your mind,
So, full of lost love and desire.

If only, I could heal your pain,
Find the lost love that made you lame.
But, the desire you feel is your own,
Can't you share with anyone?

A life of love and no pain,
Untamed desires could be our gain.
But, how can you tame the wildest of beast?
Desires of the past that cannot be released.

Love is the answer,
But you must let go,
Of untamed desires.
And thoughts of old!

Where Are the Golden Rules?

When I was young, I love to play.
Running, Jumping, staying in one place.
I grew up in just one house.
No one yelled, there was no
screaming and shouting.

As I got older, I noticed,
People moved around much more,
Children aren't as happy,
Mom is never home.

Parents leave their children all alone.
Children on street corners, Mom's working.
Children dealing drugs; Dad's away on a job.
No Prayer in school! What's wrong with that!

Where are the golden rules?

When I was young; I would never have
imagined the world, we live in today!

Full of crime, No Wonder!
Parents are hardly home! No Prayer in schools!

Who is left to install morals in our youth!

Where did you say; They put the golden rules?

Wolf from Hell

Thieves were led by the wolf from hell.
For they woke up early and destroyed our children,
And their parents while they were sleeping.

They thought they would steal our
hopes and our dreams,
But instead, they united a nation
and make us stronger!
They not only hurt our country but their own.

Brave men fight like Eagles.
Soaring until they need to fight!
They do not stalk their prey in the night.

Why is it that a "Wolf" can trick
so many into believing;
What he does is for God?
He hides like a snake in the woods,
instead of fighting himself.

What kind of leader would you follow?
One how hides and searches for his
prey in the morning hours,
Or one who soars day and night unafraid to fight!

Our God's are not so different. Our leaders are!
Our God wants peace!
It is taught throughout the Bible and the Koran.

If God wanted to punish the United States;
He could have brought down the Twin
Towers without human help.
Both book's state "God is a
vengeful and jealous God".

Why should men pretend to be God when
they use others to fight for them.
God does not need the Wolf or
Eagle to fight His battles!

MAY GOD BLESS AND PROTECT ALL
NATIONS AND THEIR PEOPLE.

World We Can't Find

You believe you live in the world,
When in fact the world lives in you.

No one has ever found a new world,
By worrying about things like you do!

Accept what comes to you totally,
So, you can appreciate everything completely.

When your mind is peaceful,
When inner energies wake-up,

A quiet mind is all you need.
To create miracles within.

Yesterday

Yesterday is gone,
Tomorrow has not yet come,
We have only today!

Live, Love and be happy

Your Imagination

If I could walk one day in your imagination.
Walk the bridges you've walked.

If I could see the skies through
the light in your eyes.
And know your every broken thought.

If only I could know how to love like you do.
I could never hate no more.

For the love, you show;
Shows everyone you know.

About the Author

This is my first book. I hope "Life Happens Poetry" helps show you the way to have faith and be strong during the good and trouble times of life. Also, to trust and lean on our Savior Jesus Christ instead of yourself.

I live with my husband of 36 years on a quiet country road in central Kentucky. We have raise 3 sons and now have 14 grandchildren. Some of these poems were inspired by my family, friends, and random people I have met along life's journey.

We live in the country on five acres mostly forest. I love meditating at our pond and walking in the forest on a warm rainy day. A few of the poems were written at the pond and in the woods while relaxing and watching the sky and seasons change.

My job of 25 years is very exciting and challenging. I work in the world of aviation quality assurance. Keeping our skies safe!

Printed in the United States
By Bookmasters